FUNFAX ™

EYEWITNESS

MINI MONSTERS

Written by Susan Mayes
Illustrated by Gary Boller

HEND
PUBLISH
©1997 HENDERSO

THE WORLD OF MINI MONSTERS

Do things that scuttle, buzz, flutter or slither give you the heebie-jeebies? Do they make you squirm with horror and delight at the same time?

BEAUTIFUL BUGS AND SLIMY SLUGS

This book reveals a multitude of mini monsters in detailed close-up, for you to study and wonder at. Things that jump and fly and sting and swarm...they're all here. We even reveal the hidden horrors of mini monsters that lurk in your home!

Why do these little beasts look the way they do? Where do they live? What do they eat? How do they protect themselves? Do they have any horrible habits? Just remember...this is their world you're looking into, so what seems odd or slightly nasty to you is really only nature at work!

INSECT BITS AND PIECES

Many people think that any small creature which creeps and crawls is called an insect; but in fact an insect is a type of creature with special characteristics. Insects have six legs, and their skeleton is on the outside of their body. Weird, huh? They have three parts to their body called the head, the thorax and the abdomen. Look at the dissected jewel beetle on the next page to see what's what.

Jewel beetle

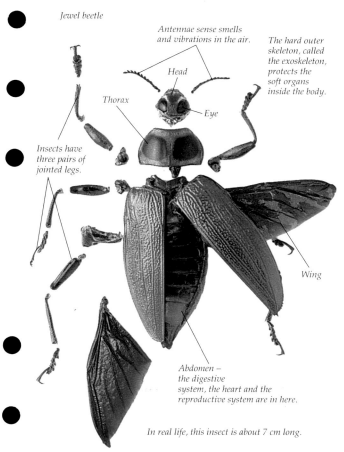

Antennae sense smells and vibrations in the air.

The hard outer skeleton, called the exoskeleton, protects the soft organs inside the body.

Head

Thorax

Eye

Insects have three pairs of jointed legs.

Wing

Abdomen – the digestive system, the heart and the reproductive system are in here.

In real life, this insect is about 7 cm long.

BELIEVE IT OR NOT...

There are at least five million insect species! There are more of this type of creature than of any other on Earth.

THE FIRST MINI MONSTERS

Insects were the first creatures ever to fly.
They lived about 300 million years ago,
even before dinosaurs! Most of the
ancient kinds are extinct now, but many
modern creepy crawlies are close relations
of the oldies.

EARLY ARRIVALS

In prehistoric times, there were brightly coloured, scented
flowers. These attracted butterflies, bees and other insects
which lived in those days. They carried pollen from
flower to flower, just as insects do today.

TRAPPED IN AMBER

We know about insects from long ago because some have
been perfectly preserved in amber. This is fossilized resin
that oozed from pine trees. Insects attracted by its
sweetness became trapped in the sticky stuff, which then
hardened and became buried for millions of years.

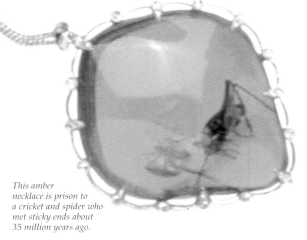

*This amber
necklace is prison to
a cricket and spider who
met sticky ends about
35 million years ago.*

ROCKY REMAINS

Some insects became trapped in muddy sediment (grains of sand, soil and plant matter) and became fossilized. Because insects are usually small and delicate, many of them rotted away before fossilization could take place, so there aren't a lot of rocky insect remains around now.

BELIEVE IT OR NOT...

This fossilized creepy crawly isn't as small as it looks here. It's a gigantic 1.8 m long. That's the size of a tall man! Yikes!

FANTASTIC FLIERS

Get this! Some ancient dragonflies may have had a wingspan of up to one metre! Most modern dragonflies are much smaller... thank goodness!

SPIDERS

Spiders are not insects. They belong to a creepy crawly group called *arachnids*. They have eight legs and two parts to their body. All spiders are carnivorous (they feed on flesh!), but not all of them make webs to catch their prey. Read on if you dare!

WONDERFUL WEBS

Some spiders make silk inside their body which they then use to spin a sticky web to catch their prey in. When an unsuspecting creature gets trapped, the spider runs out, wraps it in silk and saves it for meal time.

The common garden spider's complicated web is called an orb web.

Web silk is squeezed through nozzles called spinnerets.

SUPER STRENGTH

The silk of some webs is stronger than steel wire of the same thickness.

BELIEVE IT OR NOT...

There are about 30,000 different species of spider.

Poisonous Fangs

Most spiders stun or kill their victims with a bite from their poisonous fangs. Very few spiders are dangerous to humans though.

Fishing Net Spider

This crafty hunter spins a stretchy silk net. It hangs upside-down holding the net in its four front legs, waiting to drop it over unsuspecting victims.

Teeny Weeny Spiders

Baby spiders are called *spiderlings*. They hatch from eggs inside a silken cocoon, then cut their way out.

Big, Hairy Horrors!

Big, hairy scuttlers called tarantulas must be everybody's spider nightmare, striking fear into the heart of the bravest people. In reality it's quite a different story. Tarantulas are shy creatures which live mainly in burrows (and you thought that only rabbits did that!). However, if you're a lizard, a mouse or even a bird...watch out!

Fat feelers called pedipalps

Red-kneed tarantula

BEETLES

Beetles are the largest group of insects.
There are around 400,000 different
kinds around the world – in freezing
cold places, in scorching hot places, in
damp and muddy places – there are
beetles everywhere.

BEETLE BUFFET

Beetles eat just about anything. They dine on all kinds of
plants and animals, living and dead! They are often
thought of as pests because they attack crops, but they do
good as well, clearing up dead plants and animals.

UP, UP AND AWAY!

Beetles have four wings. The front pair are hard and
strong. They cover the beetle's back and protect the long,
folded wings underneath, which are used for flying.

BLISTER BEETLES

If the blood of a blister beetle gets on the skin of a
person or an animal, it causes painful blisters. An
excellent way of saying "leave me alone"!

WHAT A STINK!

Now don't go upsetting this one. The devil's coach-horse
beetle defends itself by arching its tail and squirting foul-
smelling liquid from its rear end. NOT a nice habit.

COLOURFUL CHARACTERS

People often think of beetles as being black, but they come in all sorts of fantastic colours. Green and red are common beetle colours, but they also come in shimmering gold, bright blue and white. Intricate patterns are another special feature of these decorative beasties.

HEAVY GIANT

An adult goliath beetle can measure as long as 15 cm (6 in). Prepare to be horrified when you check this length out on a ruler.

Goliath beetle

Bugs

The word 'bug' is often used to describe crawling insects, but the truth is that bugs are a particular kind of crawler. They have a long, hollow feeding tube which they use to pierce food and suck up the juices. Delicious! Most bugs eat plant food, but some eat live prey!

Shield Bugs

Many of these bugs have brightly-coloured patterns which look a lot like decorative shields. Shield bugs are also called stink bugs because they ooze a nasty-niffing liquid when in danger. Phewee!

Assassin Bugs

This delightful creature feeds on other insects. It stabs its victims with its feeding tube and sucks out their juices. Some South American assassin bugs feed on the blood of humans.

Assassin bug feeding

Eye Eye!

A deceptive bug this one! The front of this lantern bug's head looks like an alligator's head. When it flies, it flashes two huge false 'eyes' on its wings. These probably scare off attackers. Well it would, wouldn't it?

> Lantern bug

Baby Bugs

Baby bugs look very much like their parents, only they are smaller and have no wings. Aah!

Mind Your Toes!

Giant water bugs are common in the tropics. They are also known as toe-biters, which is a tiny bit worrying! They live underwater and feed on creatures such as snails, small fish or even frogs. So next time you go swimming in the tropics, keep your shoes on!

Slowly Does It

The water measurer is a long-legged bug that takes life easy. It moves around slowly on the surface of the water and feeds on insects which are dead or dying.

ANT ANTICS

Ants belong to a group of insects called *hymenoptera*. They are called 'social' insects because they live in groups. There can be anything from 20 to many thousands in each group, called a *colony*. Their homes are underground nests.

FANGS A LOT!

Ants have different jaw shapes, depending on what they eat. The fierce-looking bulldog ant below is a *carnivore* (meat-eater). It uses its enormous, spiky jaws, called *mandibles*, for chopping up other insects. Yum yum!

OKAY BOSS!

Each nest is begun by a single queen ant. She is the only one that lays eggs. The worker ants look after her, search for food and feed her. Big-jawed soldier ants keep enemies out of the nest.

SMELLY MESSAGES

Ants pass on messages about food, enemies and their nest in two ways. Either they make chemicals called *pheromones*, which other ants can smell, or they tap each other with their antennae to get the messages across.

DRIVING THROUGH

Driver ants move their nests from place to place. The whole colony marches along catching all the insects they can find on the way.

HONEYPOT ANTS

Honeypot ants live in semi-desert areas. In the rainy season, some of the workers are fed with water and nectar until their abdomens are huge and swollen. In the dry season, when food is scarce, the other ants feed off these living larders.

Honeypot ant

CUT AND CARRY

Parasol ants cut pieces off leaves and flowers with their sharp, pointed jaws. They struggle back to the nest with them and use them to grow a kind of fungus, which the ants then eat. Delicious!

Parasol ants

Snails (...and the odd slug)

Snails and slugs are called *gastropods*, which means 'belly foot'. Their 'belly' is really a large, flat muscular foot which can slide along. This is made easier by the slime trail which they make to help them slither smoothly.

Underneath view of a snail

Bands of muscle across the foot help push the snail forward.

Believe It or Not...

Most slugs and snails are male and female at the same time. The name for this is *hermaphrodite* – but two slugs or two snails still need to mate so that they can lay eggs.

Baby Snails

Most land snails lay eggs like little white pearls in the ground, or under rotting leaves, logs or stones. When the babies hatch out, they already have a tiny curly shell. As a snail grows, the shell grows round and round.

Uh Oh!

A snail in danger pulls its feelers in and hides its body inside its shell.

In hot weather, a snail hides in its shell and seals the opening with a plug of slime. Lovely and safe and damp!

DO NOT DISTURB

Tongues and Teeth

Most land snails and freshwater snails are *herbivores* (plant-eaters). Their long tongue, called a *radula*, is covered with tiny sharp teeth that rasp and grate up vegetation.

Now the euglandina is a snail to be reckoned with! It's a meat-eater which uses its long, sharp teeth to tear up other snails. It moves quickly when a meal is nearby and stretches out to grasp its victim. Aagh!

Believe It or Not...

The giant African snail is a monster muncher. It measures around 23 cm (9 inches) long.

This is an ordinary garden snail. What a size difference!

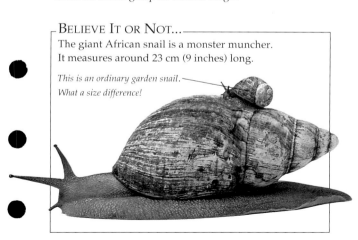

LOADS OF LEGS

If things with scuttling legs leave you feeling a little peculiar, then these pages are not for you! Introducing some many-legged mini monsters...

CATERPILLARS

Caterpillars are a bit short on legs compared with a few of the other characters shown here. They have six thin legs at the front of their bodies, some much fatter, sticky legs at the back, and two special ones called *claspers* at the very end.

WOODLICE

These shy, fourteen-legged creepers like to live where it's quite damp, so underneath logs, stones and pieces of bark are good places to hunt them out.

Woodlouse

CENTIPEDES

The name 'centipede' means 'hundred legs', but most centipedes don't have that many (although you could spend hours trying to count them!). Centipedes are fierce hunters, with a poisonous bite, so insects and worms must beware when they hear those scuttling legs.

MILLIPEDES

These many-legged beasties have soft, pale legs hidden underneath their body and a very short pair of feelers at the front. Their name means 'thousand legs', but no millipede really has that many.

There are four legs in each segment

Legs move in a wave-like pattern

Despite all these legs, millipedes meander along quite slowly.

Millipedes are plant-eaters, so they don't need to rush after food.

BELIEVE IT OR NOT...

The leggiest millipede in the world only has 710 legs. 'Thousand legs' my foot!

1. 2. 3. 4...

Leaps and Bounds

Legs are important to most creatures. Their uses include walking, running, digging, fighting and, of course, jumping. Here are a few of the mini monsters whose long legs help them to leap and bound around.

Leaping Locust

Look at the legs on this beastie. It's a locust and it's getting ready to leap. Its back legs are folded, ready for the high jump.

The locust's powerful leg muscles straighten out its leg joints and launch it into the air. Its wings stay closed to keep the body streamlined, so the locust can get as high as possible.

When it can go no higher, the locust opens its wings as wide as it can and flaps them to carry it even further forward.

To help it land safely, the locust spreads its legs wide, tilts its hind wings and curves its front ones. This helps it to slow down and drop gently to the ground.

FROG BEETLE

The frog beetle's back legs are long and strong, like a frog's. It uses them to leap away from enemies, then it uses its wings to fly to complete safety.

FIT AS A FLEA

Fleas are famous jumpers. They can leap as high as 30 cm (12 in). If you think that this doesn't sound very high, consider the size of a flea. That really is some high jump for a tiny creature.

HOT AND BOTHERED

The desert cricket uses its strong legs for long leaps, but it also uses them for digging. If it needs to escape from enemies or the raging heat of the midday sun, it digs speedily into the sand. It can bury itself in only a few seconds. Beat that!

Flea

Desert cricket

EATING OUT

Mini monsters have different feeding habits. Some can eat almost anything, while others have more specialised dietary requirements. Their feeding parts suit the sort of food they dine on.

WEEVILS

Weevils have a long, curved snout called a *rostrum*. It has tiny jaws at the end for biting small pieces of plant.

TONGUE-TIED

Butterflies and moths have a long, tube-shaped mouth called a *proboscis*. They hover in front of a flower to feed, stretch out their proboscis and delve inside for the sweet nectar. When they are not feeding, the proboscis is coiled up out of the way. Thank goodness for that!

Just look at the length of this hawk-moth's tongue!

WOW!

TWO SETS OF CHOMPERS

Ground beetles have two pairs of jaws. One huge pair is for chopping up worms, slugs and other yummy goodies. A smaller pair is for shovelling the bits into the beetle's mouth.

AN IRON GRIP

The praying mantis grips its prey with its front legs and uses its sharp, strong jaws for slicing it up.

A Quick Slurp

The darkling beetle lives in the desert. To get a drink, it waits until dew from early morning mist collects on its back. Then it holds its abdomen up so that the water drips down into its mouth. What a performance!

A Trail of Destruction

Caterpillars chew their way around the edges of a leaf. They grasp it between their legs, stretch out their head, then chew down towards their body. Look at the progress this common mormon caterpillar has made on a leaf. Hungry, or what?

This is all that's left of the leaf after eight hours.

Yucky Habits

If you're about to munch on a tasty snack while reading these pages, a word of warning... DON'T! Some of these yucky mini monster habits will make you feel distinctly peculiar!

House Flies

Do you ever see flies lurking around your kitchen? Well this is what they are up to.

Spongy mouthpart

Taste buds are on the feet

When a fly smells food, it lands and tastes it with the taste buds on its feet. If it fancies the food, it spreads digestive juices on it – rather like vomiting, actually! This turns solid food mushy, so the fly can dab it up with its sponge-like mouthparts. That's the last time you leave food uncovered!

Germs Galore!

A mosquito feasts on blood. When it bites someone, it slurps up some of their blood, plus any germs that are in it. Then it flies on to someone else and has another meal, leaking some of the germs from the first person into the new one. This spreads the germs that cause disease.

DUNG FLIES

A dung fly lays its eggs in fresh droppings. When the maggots hatch out, they eat the dung. Apparently, this contains lots of nourishment for them!

CAVE COCKROACH

Cockroaches that live in caves banquet on a tasty selection of morsels. They are particularly partial to bat droppings and the remains of dead bats. Other fine food includes mites and fungi.

LIVE FOOD

The weevil-hunting wasp grasps, stings and paralyses weevils, but doesn't kill them. The female puts the weevils in a burrow, and lays her eggs on them. When the larvae hatch, they eat the live weevils' flesh. Ouch!

The wasp holds the weevil in position with its strong legs.

DEADLY BEASTIES

If, by some strange chance, you happen to come across any of the little horrors shown here (fairly unlikely!), the best thing you could do is RUN AWAY! They are DEADLY!

BLACK WIDOW

The female black widow spider has a bite which can kill a person. She sometimes kills her mate. Nice habit, eh?

SAHARA SCORPION

Scorpions are eight-legged relatives of spiders. They only sting to protect themselves. The Sahara scorpion is only 7 cm (2.8 in) long, but its sting is strong enough to kill you. So steer clear next time you're in the Sahara desert!

Sahara scorpion

POISONOUS SNAILS

Many seashells you find on the beach are the empty homes of sea snails. The cone shell lurks on coral reefs and stabs its prey with a poisonous dart which paralyses and kills. A number of humans have met a sticky end in this way.

The geography cone is highly poisonous.

PRETTY DEADLY

Just in case you happen to be trekking through the jungle one day, watch out for these cute, pretty little frogs. They are called poison dart frogs. A smear of their poison can kill a human, so HANDS OFF!

This little cutie is the world's most poisonous frog.

IF YOU'RE A MALE PRAYING MANTIS...

A special warning for YOU. Beware of those crafty females you're so fond of! If they're hungry, they may eat males like you while mating.

The female is bigger than the male.

Flying High

One of the main reasons why insects have survived for millions of years is that they can fly. Their wings help them to escape from danger, find food and places to live.

What's In a Wing?

An insect's wings are thin and light. (Well, heavy ones wouldn't be very useful, would they?) They are stiffened by a network of veins. The flapping power comes from strong muscles in the insect's middle.

Getting Warm

Before an insect's wings can move fast enough to fly, the flight muscles need to be warmed up, especially when the weather is cool.

Mini Helicopters

Hoverflies can move forwards, backwards, sideways, up and down, just like a helicopter. As their name suggests, they can also hover in midair. Very few insects can perform this stunt.

Gliding By

Some insects have wings specially made for gliding long distances. The African grasshopper has broad hind wings made for this job.

BEAUTIFUL BUTTERFLIES

Lots of tropical butterflies are big and bright. They avoid hungry enemies by darting in and out of patches of sunlight and dark, shadowy places. This makes them difficult to see.

Australian hercules moth

WONDERFUL WINGS

The Australian hercules moth has a larger wing area than any other insect. Its wingspan (from wingtip to wingtip) is 28 cm (11 in). That's some flutterer!

BELIEVE IT OR NOT...

The fastest ever flier was probably a giant prehistoric dragonfly. These huge insects probably had to fly as fast as 69 km/h (43 mph) just to stay up in the air!

EYE SPY

Most insects are tiny, but they have more developed senses than most larger animals. They can see and hear things that humans cannot detect.

Caterpillars are surrounded by their food, so they don't need to look hard to find it. They can make do with simple eyes.

SIMPLE EYES

Insects which do not need sharp eyesight have eyes called *simple eyes*. These can probably only see light and shade, and not much more.

COMPOUND EYES

Now we're talking super-vision here. Beasties with *compound eyes* have excellent eyesight.

Compound eyes are made up of lots of separate sections, called *ommatidia*. The more of these there are, the more sensitive the eye is.

HUGE EYES

A dragonfly's eyes take up most of its head. This means that it can see in front, above, below and behind, all at the same time. It's no good sneaking up on a dragonfly – it'll see you coming!

Dragonfly's head

LOTS OF EYES

Many insects have simple eyes AND compound eyes. The wasp and the cicada both have compound eyes and three simple eyes.

Wasp

Simple eyes

Compound eyes

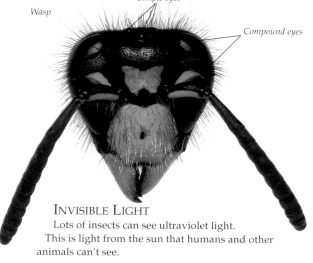

INVISIBLE LIGHT

Lots of insects can see ultraviolet light. This is light from the sun that humans and other animals can't see.

Some flowers have petals with lines which reflect ultraviolet light. To an insect, this makes the lines look like bright runways guiding them right into the middle of the flower, where all the yummy pollen and nectar is.

HUNTING SPIDERS

Spiders which hunt for their prey have really sharp eyesight. Well they should really, because they have eight eyes to spy what's happening! This helps them to stalk their victims and pounce on them.

Touch, Smell and Hearing

Bodies of insects have lots of short hairs connected to the nervous system. These can feel tiny vibrations in the air made by sound and movement. Some hairs can even sense smells and flavours.

Fringed Feelers

Insects' antennae often have sensory hairs for feeling. The Indian beetle has huge fringed antennae to help it pick up scents in the air. Beetles fan out their antennae when they fly, to help them to smell as much as possible.

The Indian beetle's giant antennae look like antlers.

Feathered Sensor

A male gypsy moth's big, feathered antennae are so sensitive that they can smell the scent of a female gypsy moth from far away. Moths can also tell different flowers and plants apart by their smells.

FEELING TOUCHY
Because many insects rely on touch and smell so much, they usually have small eyes, but very long antennae. The longhorn beetle has a fine pair of feelers which are jointed, so they can be moved around.

A longhorn beetle with its antennae pointing backwards.

SEEING IN THE DARK
Insects that live in the dark have to use other ways of 'seeing'. The cave cricket lives in dark caves and feels the world around it with its long antennae.

BELIEVE IT OR NOT...
A cricket hears with its legs. Yes...really! Its ears are a swelling just below the knee on each front leg.

Doing Battle

Many mini monsters attack and kill the creepy crawlies they feed on. But some beasties fight their own kind to protect their territory and to compete for food and places to mate.

Battling Bees

Every bee colony has its own scent. If a bee from another colony tries to get into the hive, the others recognize that the intruder smells different and push it out. The intruder may curl up, telling the other bees "I give in".

The Tale of the Lost Ant

Imagine the scene...your pet cat is basking in the sunshine when an ant crawls on to its fur. Moggy gets up, stretches and wanders to another part of the neighbourhood, where the ant gets off. Far from home, the ant tries to join another colony of ants. MISTAKE! The ants can smell that it's a stranger and kill it. THE END!

WHO'S BOSS?

Stag beetles compete for the dead wood that they feed and breed on. The males have big jaws which look like antlers, rather like the antlers of a real stag. They use these weapons for wrestling.

When two males meet, they stretch out their antennae to pick up lots of information about each other. Each male takes up a threatening pose to try to frighten off his opponent.

If threats don't work, each beetle tries to grip his rival around the middle, to lift him up and drop him to the ground. Sometimes, the teeth on the jaws of the winning beetle puncture the loser's tough armour.

Stag beetles

An injured beetle will probably die, especially if it lands on its back. This can be particularly bad news if there are ants around, because they enjoy a tasty beetle for supper!

FINDING A MATE

For most creepy crawlies, a female has to mate with a male of her own kind before she can lay eggs. Finding the right mate, avoiding being eaten and laying the eggs in a safe place is full of hazards.

MOTH MATES

A moth's antennae are so sensitive to smells that it can smell the scent of a mate from far away. The Indian moon moth can smell a mate from a distance of over 11 km (6 1/4 miles) away.

Indian moon moth

CHIRPING GRASSHOPPERS

A grasshopper makes a chirping sound to attract a mate. It does this by rubbing its back leg along its front wing. This makes small teeth on the leg buzz.

COURTSHIP DANCES

Just to make sure that they have found the right species to mate with, butterflies perform dancing flights. While they dance, they exchange scented chemical signals, called *pheromones*, telling them that the partner they have found is the one for them. Aaah!

LIGHTING UP

Glow-worms have nothing whatsoever to do with worms. They are the wingless females of particular kinds of beetle! At night, the female makes a light near the tip of her abdomen. This attracts males who come and mate with her. Some kinds of glow-worm even flash a code to attract a mate. Smart, eh?

Empid flies

GORGEOUS GIFTS

In some species where insects feed on other insects, the male gives the female a gift of food when they mate, so that she doesn't eat HIM! A tasty dead insect seems to do the trick for some females. Well, they would be mad to turn down such a special present... wouldn't they?

ALL CHANGE

For us humans, growing up is quite straightforward compared with growing up for insects. We are born, then we grow until we become adults. But insects go through stages where their body shape changes completely, several times, before they make it to the 'grown-up' stage.

This is called *complete metamorphosis* (which means a complete change).

BUTTERFLIES

A female butterfly lays its eggs on a plant.

The eggs hatch into a squidgy-looking creature called a *larva*. A butterfly larva is called a caterpillar.

Chrysalis

Chrysalis skin splits

Next, the caterpillar becomes something called a *pupa*, or *chrysalis*. To do this, its caterpillar skin splits to reveal its chrysalis skin underneath. The chrysalis hangs from a branch or under a leaf.

Inside the chrysalis, the butterfly's shape is forming. Many chrysalises look like old leaves. NOT very pretty!

After a few weeks the butterfly emerges from the chrysalis skin. This process takes about 20 minutes of hard work. The beautiful, new creature waits for its wings to harden properly, and then flies off to find its first meal.

LITTLE BY LITTLE

Some insects don't go through as many stages as others. They hatch from their eggs into babies called *nymphs*, which look like tiny adults.

The nymphs moult their outer skins many times, changing body size a bit each time. This is called *incomplete metamorphosis*. Insects that grow up this way include grasshoppers, cockroaches and dragonflies.

PHEW!
I'M A GROWN-UP AT LAST.

STINGING THINGS

If you've ever been stung by a mini monster, you'll know that it's not very pleasant! Here are some beasties with a sting in the tail.

BEES

Bees are plant-eaters, so the sharp sting in their tail is nothing to do with killing prey for food – it's for scaring off enemies. But give a moment's thought to this poor little buzzer. When it stings something, the sting and part of the body tears away and the bee dies.

WASPS

These beasties can use their sting several times, so beware! They use them for killing prey and to protect themselves. Wasps do some good though, because they kill creatures that destroy plants and fruit.

BELIEVE IT OR NOT...

About 40,000 people are killed each year by wasp or bee stings because of allergic reactions.

THE BIGGEST WASP

The tarantula hawk wasp is the world's biggest wasp.
Its wingspan is about 12 cm (5 in). Aagh!

The female captures a big spider and paralyses it with
her sting. She then lays an egg on it and pushes it into
a small burrow.

When the wasp grub hatches out, it feeds on the living,
paralysed spider. Live food...
mmm-mmmmm!

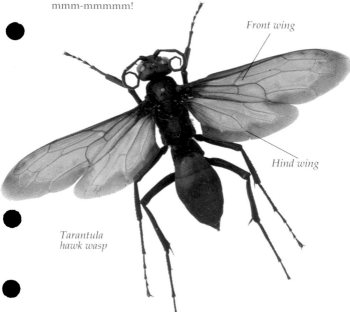

Front wing

Hind wing

*Tarantula
hawk wasp*

BUTTERFLY HUNTER

A type of South American wasp attacks groups of
butterflies sitting on the ground and collects them to make
a food store for its grubs when they hatch out. After
stinging the butterflies, one at a time, it bites their wings
off. Nice little creature!

FALSE ID

Being any sort of small creature can be a dangerous business, so many little beasties have special ways of staying safe. They have sneaky ways of hiding, or they masquerade as something much more frightening.

CAMOUFLAGE

Some insects have body colouring that matches their background, making them almost impossible to see. This works best of all if they keep still...the slightest fidget and they could become supper to a hungry hunter.

Can you spot the Indian leaf butterfly? It looks just like an old leaf.

Butterfly's head

Butterfly's wing

Bottom of wing

Another type of camouflage called *disruptive coloration* disguises the body by breaking its shape up with stripes and areas of colour.

IN DISGUISE

Many insects mimic (copy) the shapes and colours of things far more dangerous to scare their enemies away.

The hoverfly isn't dangerous, but it looks it because its colouring and pattern is the same as a wasp's. Handy, eh?

The eyed hawk-moth gets its name from the big spots on its hind wings. They look like frightening, staring eyes.

Hoverfly

HAHA!

HOUSEHOLD HORRORS

If you thought that your home was a mini monster-free zone...WRONG!   Most homes have some sort of hidden creepy crawly life. Hopefully, yours won't have most of these though.

COCKROACHES

These beasties are ancient insects. They live almost anywhere and eat just about everything. They can become household pests, eating any food which is left around. Their flattened bodies make it easy for them to hide in cracks, so they are difficult to get rid of.

BEDBUGS

Now these will have you scratching! Bedbugs are bloodsucking bugs. They mostly live in birds' nests and where bats roost, but they also live IN YOUR HOME! They reproduce quickly in warm conditions, so a nice warm bedroom – your mattress in particular – will make a wonderfully comfortable residence for them.

Bedbugs in close-up

Real size of a bedbug

HOUSEFLIES

Every country has houseflies. These excellent fliers love to hang around your home looking for food, and they are not fussy about the quality of it either. Old leftovers will do just fine, thank you!

WASPS

Wasps often make their nests in the roofs of houses, where it's warm and safe. Ideal for the wasps maybe, but not for the humans they share the house with. Bzzzzzzzzzzz!

FLEAS

Each kind of flea prefers the blood of one sort of animal or bird. The bad news is that fleas can be smuggled into your home on an innocent pet. The good news is that animal fleas have to be very hungry to attack a human.

A flea bite leaves you with an itchy red spot. Beware of madly scratching pets!

HEAD LICE

These tiny terrors can live in human hair. They grip on tightly and puncture the skin with their mouthparts, so they can suck up blood. Eeeeek!

DEATHWATCH BEETLE

These beetles feed on the wood of oak trees. They are the dreaded enemies of people who live in houses with oak timbers, as they munch away on the wood. This weakens the framework of the house.

NESTS

Some insects live on their own (oh, poor things), but others live together in groups, or *societies*. They are called *social insects* and they build nests where they protect each other and bring up their babies. How civilized!

WASPS

The boss of a wasp colony is the queen. In the spring she begins a new nest made from chewed-up wood. She builds a few cells for her eggs.

The queen builds more paper layers around the cells to make an extra safe and warm home.

Inside, the queen lays a single egg in each cell. When the larvae hatch out, the queen feeds them with tasty morsels of caterpillar.

The first lot of babies grow up and become workers. They gather food for the next lot of larvae. By summer, the nest may have as many as 500 wasps inside. Yikes!

ANTS

Different kinds of ants build different kinds of nests. Wood ants build enormous ones from the remains of plants. Inside, there is a complicated network of tunnels where all the ants live.

TERMITES

Termites are social insects that look and live like ants. They have the most complicated insect societies and build huge nests to live in. The nests can last for several years.

This African termites' nest has umbrella-like layers, but nobody knows why.

BELIEVE IT OR NOT...

The tallest termite nests are made by the African termite. They can measure an amazing 12.8 m (42 ft) high. That's as high as seven tall people standing on top of each other!

Monster Monsters

Some creepers, slitherers and flutterers are small and sweet-looking, but some are HUGE. Well, that's HUGE when they are sitting next to their small relations. Here are a few of the unbelievably BIG beasties that you really ought to know about.

The Longest Insect
Stick insects are the longest insects in the world. African ones can be as long as 40 cm (15 3/4 in).

The Longest Antennae
The proud owner of the longest antennae is the New Guinea longhorn beetle. Its fantastic feelers are 20 cm (7 1/2 in) long.

The Longest Centipede
At 33 cm (13 in) in length, a centipede found on the Andaman Islands in the Bay of Bengal is the longest one on record. It measured almost 4 cm (1 1/2 in) wide.

Yikes! That's a long, skinny scuttler!

THE LONGEST MILLIPEDE
Two kinds of millipede from the Seychelles measure as long as 28 cm (11 in).

THE HEAVIEST INSECT
Goliath beetles can weigh up to 100 g. That's as much as two Funfax books!

THE LARGEST LAND SNAIL
Imagine this if you can. The largest recorded land snail measured 39.3 cm (15 1/2 in) from tip to toe. What a slime trail that slitherer must have left!

THE LARGEST DRAGONFLY
A dragonfly from Central and South America measures up to 12 cm (4 3/4 in) across its wings and 19 cm (7 1/2 in) in length.

THE LARGEST SPIDER
The goliath bird-eating spider is ENORMOUS! One has been found with a leg-span of 28 cm (11 in). Scary, or what?

THE LARGEST BUTTERFLY
The Queen Alexandra's birdwing butterfly is the largest known butterfly in the world. Its wingspan measures an incredible 28 cm (11 in). Imagine those wings brushing against your face! Aaaagh!

INDEX

Acknowledgements: (KEY: t=top, b=bottom/below, c=centre, l=left, r=right)
Gary Staab (model-maker): back cover tr

Picture Credits: American Museum of Natural History/OW Myers: 25c;
NHPA/Stephen Dalton: 10b; Oxford Scientific Films/Kathie Atkinson: 12c;
/Densey Clyne: 13c; /James Robinson: front cover cl.

Additional Photography: Jane Burton, Andy Crawford, Geoff Dann,
Angelika Elsebach, Frank Greenaway, Mark Ilcy, Colin Keates, Dave King,
Stephen Oliver, Harry Taylor, Jerry Young.

Every effort has been made to trace the copyright holders. Henderson
Publishing Ltd apologises for any unintentional omissions and would be
pleased, in such cases, to add an acknowledgement in further editions.

Use the flea sticker on the fold-out Time Line in your Funfax Eyewitness Library. See inside cover for details.